Raising Creative Kids

A Collection of Simple Creativity Prompts for Children

Colleen Kessler

ISBN-13: 978-1503056947

ISBN-10: 1503056945

DEDICATION

For my own four creative kids -- Trevor, Molly, Logan, and Isaac. Thanks for challenging me every day to find ways to stretch your imaginations and learn alongside you. You're such wonderfully imaginative explorers, and I adore spending my days with you!

CONTENTS

How to Use This Book

I'm so glad you picked up this book and are as excited as I am about fostering creativity in children. You may be a homeschooler like me, send your kids to public school, have children in parochial or private schools, or do some kind of mix of schooling.

It doesn't matter.

Really... we are all concerned parents who understand that creative, imaginative, and flexible thinking is crucial to growing a generation of world-changers. And, it's up to us to make sure our kids get opportunities to kick-start their imaginations. STEAM {Science, Technology, Engineering, Arts, and Mathematics} is the way of the future and we need to nurture that mind-set in our kids. They need to play with the what-ifs.

Because I know kids are all different, and this IS a book about creativity, I'm going to encourage you to use it in your own way. If you have the eBook, print the pages on cardstock — two to a page — and cut them in half. Draw from them when you need inspiration. Add the book to your child's

routine. Every day, have him or her choose an activity from the print or Kindle book, and do it —
inviting siblings, neighbors, and friends to play along. Big, small, whatever, any child can play make-
believe no matter their age. They just need encouragement and a loving place to play.

There's so much fun to be had; why not try some of these with your child yourself? I'd love to see
pictures of your kids getting creative, and invite you to share your photos on the RLL Facebook
page { facebook.com/RaisingLifelongLearners } tagged #RaisingCreativeKids. I just might share the
photo on the website, or the main Facebook page — I love creativity at work!

Above all, and in everything you do, enjoy those precious children. They are beautiful gifts to be
cherished. Have fun!

The pretend play of childhood is often just considered valueless fun. The truth is, though, the ability to turn an ordinary bedroom into a princess's private quarters or a soldier's bunker takes critical thinking, problem solving, coordination, cooperation, and a great deal of flexibility in thinking.

Imaginative play offers many benefits for children.

Through pretend play children:

- work out their confusing, scary, or unknown situations. For example, by playing doctor and giving shots, children can demystify the whole "getting a check-up" thing.
- learn about themselves and the world in which they live. Have you ever seen a child acting out a family? Or making dinner in a pretend kitchen? Or being the grocer in a game? These activities all help them know who they are and how they fit into their world.
- develop higher order thinking skills. Pretend play requires complex social skills and communication. Kids learn to negotiate, consider other children's solutions, and transfer knowledge from one situation to another. They learn to delay gratification and to compromise.
- cultivate social and emotional intelligence. Interacting with others is a crucial life skill, and by engaging in imaginative play with others, kids work on this in a tangible and life-skills developing way.
- synthesize knowledge and skills. When they play in the toy kitchen, they sort and classify food, prepare it according to how they've seen mom or dad do it, organize their thinking and serve the meal.

As a parent or caregiver, you can facilitate this type of play and learning by telling your children stories, providing them with dolls, puppets, and other props, and encouraging them to stretch their thinking.

Children's days are getting more and more structured, but it's important to think about what they're missing out on if they're not getting unstructured time to play. In many ways, a few hours of cops and robbers, princesses and paupers, or other games, is as developmentally important as any art class or sports team. Allow time for fort building, don't rush them through schoolwork or chores, and jump in to don a pith helmet of your own and wield a sword to protect your queen – you and your child will be better off for it.

Colleen Kessler

Make a Pirate Ship

Use things from around the house — blankets, chairs, tables, boxes, cartons, wood — to build a pirate ship. Outfit it with cannons, and make your own flag to fly from the mast. Don't forget to make a walking plank.

Practice your AAARRRGGGGGHHHH and other pirate words before embarking on your trip through the   Seven Seas to plunder and pillage.

Then... set sail, me heartys!

Have a Dance Party

Gather your dress up clothes, scarves, and headdresses… it's time to dance! Make a disco ball out of tin foil, string some fairy lights throughout the house, and crank up the music.

While you're at it, invent some new dance moves of your own.

Make a Restaurant

Set-up tables and chairs, drape them with cloth, and set them in a pretty way. Make up a menu {real or imagined}, and invite your guests to opening night. Make sure you are dressed for success on the grand opening of your new business. Take orders, serve food, and maybe set yourself a part from all of the other restaurants out there with awesome entertainment.

What is your restaurant called?

The Evening News

It's time for the evening news. What's happening around your neighborhood? With the weather? Around the country?

Pull out weather maps {Mom, printables abound on the Internet} , shirts and ties, and stacks of "story notes." Come up with a news desk, studio, and camera setup and assign jobs. This is a great thing for big kids and little kids to do together!

When you're ready, tell your parents to "tune in." It's time for the news.

Pizza Delivery

Dinner time on a busy evening calls for pizza delivery. Gather materials — an old pizza box {restaurants will usually give you one}, toppings cut from felt or paper, dough {paper plate, playdough, etc.}, and have someone call in an order.

Prepare your customer's pizza and get set to deliver. How will you get it there nice and hot? By plane, train, car, or truck? Hovercraft? Only your imagination will limit you.

Emergency!

Cardboard box time — grab a big one, and be creative in turning it into a fire truck, ambulance, or a police car. {Or make all three.} Markers, crayons, construction paper, tissue paper... use whatever you have on hand.

Now, what is the emergency? Do you have a dispatcher to call the squads out? Perhaps a donut truck rolled over on the highway. You'll need the police to direct traffic, and the fire and rescue squads to assess for injuries. {And maybe some napkins to wipe sugary donut fingertips.}

Art Show

It's time to unleash your inner Monet, Picasso, Degas, or Cassatt. Paint, chalk, color, or collage a collection of art work. Make frames and title cards for your displays.

Tape your framed work around the house and whip up some appetizers and uncork some sparkling cider. Invite all of the art patrons you know and love.

Dress in your finest artist clothes, and prepare to dazzle everyone with your talent, poise, and conversation...and sell all of your work — after all, artists need to eat too, right?

Colleen Kessler

Post Office

Time to deliver the mail — but first it needs to be written! Write letters to friends, neighbors, and family members. Make a large mailbox using a cardboard box, and smaller mailboxes using cereal, shoe, or other small boxes. Put them around the neighborhood or around your house. Encourage others to write letters and place them in the large community mailbox to be delivered.

Then strap on your mailbag and get to work. Remember, the post office delivers in any weather, so get the job done. People need their mail, after all!

Coffee Shop

Have you ever gone for coffee with your mom or dad?
There are interesting people in coffee shops... Writers
working on their next novel, artists sketching a new
painting idea, moms with toddlers and babies out for an
afternoon break, businessmen meeting clients,
grandmas, grandpas, teens, and really, anyone in
between.

Set up your own coffee shop. What will you serve?
What's it called? Will you be a worker? A patron? What
kinds of people do you see when you look around?
Which type of coffee shop customer would you be?

Travel Time

You need to go on a trip — around the world, across the country, to Disneyland, or to the next town over to see Grandma. How will you get there?

Design your transportation using a cardboard box. Will it be a plane? A train? A car? A camper? Who will drive? What will the service personnel serve for snacks or meals? Will you need to sleep on board? How long will the trip take? Do you need to use multiple means of transportation to get to your destination? You have only the limits of your own imagination — so explore!

Creativity involves the imagination, but furthers its application to develop science and math skills in children. When kids are encouraged to think creatively, they employ the use of the scientific method, communication skills, fine and gross motor planning, problem solving and posing, as well as using basic literacy skills like using symbols and inferring what others are thinking or hypothesizing what may or may not work in a given situation.

You can help your child develop fluency in thinking by posing open-ended questions and challenges. This stimulates their thinking and allows for cognitive growth.

Encourage them to be flexible and approach problems and challenges from multiple perspectives. Allow them to explore and experiment.

Ask them for other ways to solve the same problem, or give them the challenge again – this time with a different set of materials.

Encourage your child's originality by asking them for new and novel ways to approach old problems. Then, have them elaborate on their solutions – what else could they do? How would that make it better?

Above all, have fun and encourage your child to have fun discovering, experimenting, and tinkering.

Raising Creative Kids: A Collection of Simple Creativity Prompts for Children

Tallest Tower

Let's see how creative you can be with just a few simple materials. You'll need 30 drinking straws, a foot of masking tape, 10 rubber bands, a pair of scissors, and a piece of computer printer paper.

Grab a timer and set it for 20 minutes. That's how long you have to use only the materials you've gathered to build the tallest free-standing tower possible. That means it has to stand on its own. No fair taping it to the floor or leaning it against something.

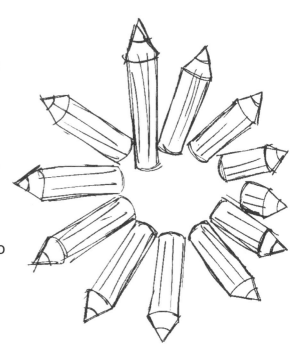

Pendulum Painting

Have you ever seen a pendulum? It's a weight that's hung from a fixed point, but can swing freely back and forth.

Make a pendulum using a plastic cup and a piece of string. Tie it to a fixed point like a hanging light or have someone hold it steady for you. Poke a small hole in the bottom of the cup, put a large piece of art paper on a table underneath your pendulum, and fill the cup with paint. Set your pendulum in motion.

What do you notice about the "picture" you are painting? Can you add another paint color and set it in motion again? And again?

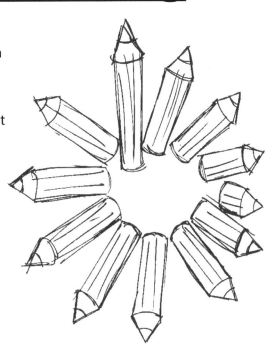

Planet Persimmon

You've just discovered a new planet, and named it Planet Persimmon because of its unusually orange color, tomato-like shape, and sweet smell.

Exploring Planet Persimmon is lots of fun, but you keep seeing this strange creature following you. What is it? What does it look like? What will you name it {after all, you discovered the place}? What does it eat?

Make this native Persimmonian animal out of clay. Write a report or story about it, giving details about its life, habits, and needs.

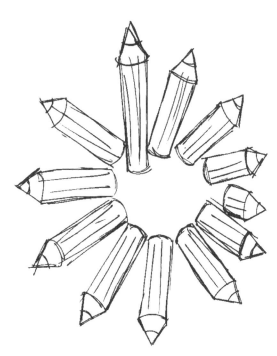

Marshmallow City

Building play you can eat… awesome! Grab a bag of marshmallows {and maybe a bag of mini marshmallows, too} and some toothpicks. Now, build the world's first city made out of marshmallows. What does your city need to thrive? Will there be a police station? Marshmallow people? A school, playground, or pool?

Maybe not a pool…water and marshmallows don't mix well.

Tell an adult all about your city. Then eat it. Yum!

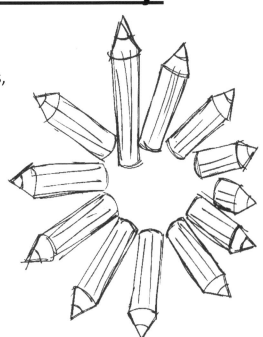

The Best Boat Ever

Find these materials: a sheet of aluminum foil {about 12-inches long}, a piece of paper, a roll of masking tape, 20 drinking straws, a pair of scissors, and a big jar of pennies.

Set a timer for 20 minutes — that's how long you have to complete this challenge...go!

Build a super-strong boat, one that will hold an incredible amount of pennies before sinking to the bottom of your bathtub. When it's built, test it out, adding the pennies one at a time. How many did it take to sink it? Do you think you can build one that will hold more?

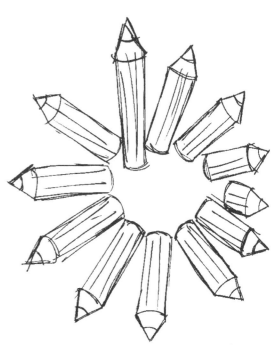

Unusual Painting Materials

Do you usually paint with a paintbrush? Have you ever tried to use something different? Experiment.

Drop paint on paper and run toy cars and trains through it. What do you notice? Which makes the most unusual pattern?

Now try using marbles, cotton balls, pom poms, balloons, Q-tips, toy animals, bubble wrap, plastic wrap, crumpled foil, and anything else you have handy in your recycle bin.

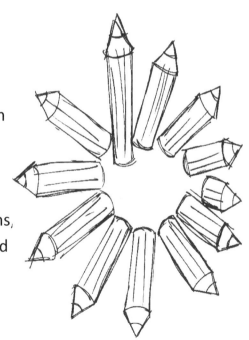

Beautiful Feet

Women pierce their ears and pin in pretty earrings. They paint their faces with make-up, and drape necklaces, rings, and bracelets on. Men wear rings and neck chains, and take care to dress well, too.

Have you ever wondered why not very many people pay attention to their feet?

Today, use washable paint or make-up and decorate your feet. Paint your toenails, add glitter, draw patterns and designs. Wrap handmade bracelets around your ankles. Choose your prettiest shoes. Go on a fashion walk around the house or neighborhood.

Crazy Kitchen Concoctions

Time for Mom and Dad to get out of the kitchen! Go through the refrigerator and cupboards and plan a no-cook breakfast, lunch, dinner, or snack.

Here's the catch...

It needs to be made up of things that you wouldn't normally put together. It's time to get crazy with combinations. Ever wonder what chocolate drizzled cheese sticks would taste like? Now's your chance to find out.

Invite the family to sample your crazy concoction when it's ready... Remind your family that the polite thing to do at every meal is to try at least a bite of everything.

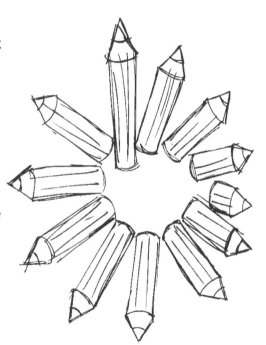

Create an Animal

Go for a nature walk and collect fallen things like sticks, leaves, rocks, moss, and anything else that look interesting. Bring your finds back home and spread them out at the kitchen table.

Now, get constructing… use the materials you have gathered to create a new animal. Collage, build, suspend, imagine, and put the materials together in any way you want.

Once your creature is "born," decide where it lives, what it eats, how it protects itself, and what it's called Then introduce it to the rest of your family.

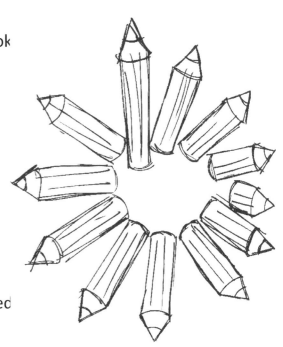

The Strongest Bridge

Grab 30 drinking straws, 15 craft sticks, 3 feet of masking tape, 2 sheets of notebook paper, and a pair of scissors.

Set a timer for 20 minutes. During that time, build the strongest bridge you possibly can. Make sure that it is free-standing and can support weight up off the ground.

Then test it. Set one toy car after another onto the bridge to see how many it can hold before it collapses. Once you know the results, gather the same materials and try again — this time making one that holds even more.

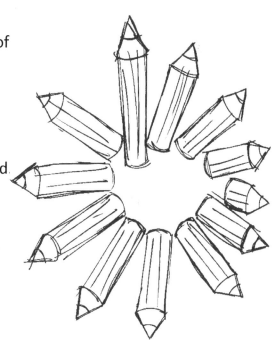

Experimentation is crucial in young children – whether it's art, science, literacy, motor skills, or whatever. Kids need to be given the opportunity to look at a circumstance, predict what the outcome may be, then experiment to see if what they thought comes to be... and then analyze the results.

These simple processes help develop reasoning and critical thinking skills, and teach children to question, describe, test, explain, and communicate well. Children with these skills grow to be leaders and world changers because they learn from the start not to take things at face value.

They learn to take an active part in their world.

Colleen Kessler

Play with Your Food

Have you ever wondered about the properties of certain foods? Like... what would happen if a banana was frozen in its peel. And, then what would happen if it was left on the counter to thaw. Try it.

If you don't have a science journal, this would be a good time to start one. Write or draw what you think might happen, what you're going to do, and then step-by-step what you end up doing.

Finally, record your results in words and/or pictures. Then try it with other types of food.

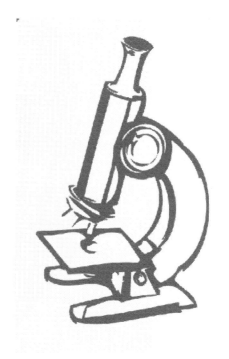

Colleen Kessler

Amazing Reactions

All foods are either acids or bases. Do you know what happens when you put a few teaspoons of baking soda into a cup of vinegar? A chemical reaction causes the vinegar to bubble and rise. Vinegar is an acid and baking soda is a base. The two cause a reaction together. Try it out.

Then, try adding a few teaspoons of your base {baking soda} to different liquids in your kitchen like apple juice, milk, soda pop, water, etc.

Decide which are acids and which are bases by analyzing their reactions.

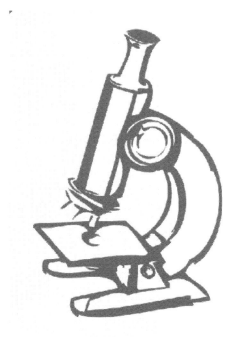

Let's Concentrate

Ask your mom to pick up a container of apple juice and another of frozen apple juice concentrate from the store.

Compare the two. Taste them both. Smell them. How are they similar? Different? Jot your thoughts down in your science notebook.

Now... put a tablespoon of apple juice concentrate in a glass. Predict how many tablespoons of water it will take to dilute the concentrate enough that it tastes like the juice your mom bought.

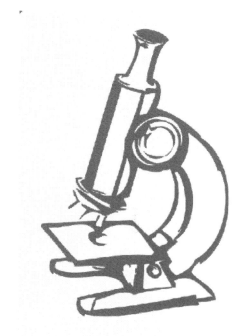

Icy Explorations

Dump a pile of ice onto a tray. Observe, and write about its properties in your science journal. What does it feel like? Does it bounce or roll? Does it have a smell? Etc.

Is there a way to get that ice to melt really quickly? Do you think an ice cube will melt faster with hot water poured on it, with cold water poured on it, with salt dumped on it, or if left alone?

Try it out and record your results in your journal.

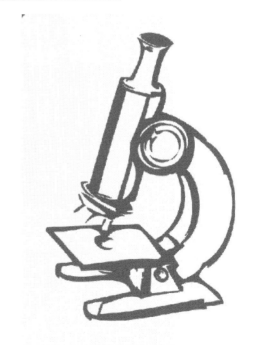

Whipped Soap

Pour a small bottle of dish soap into a mixing bowl. How does it smell? What does it look like? How does it feel?

What do you think will happen if you beat it with a hand mixer? Will its properties change? How?

Try it.

What happened? Record your observations in your science journal.

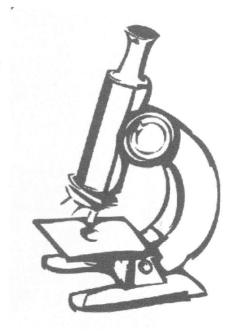

Insulate It

Take four ice cubes out of the freezer and place them on a tray. How fast do you think they will melt if left out on the table? Depending on the temperature, it could happen pretty quickly, right?

Try this... hypothesize how you might keep the ice solid for longer. Use different materials to make an insulator around each cube, leaving one out as the control cube. Now, predict which one will melt the slowest and take note of the time. Check back every ten minutes or so and write down the time when you notice one is melted. Continue until they are all melted. Was your guess correct?

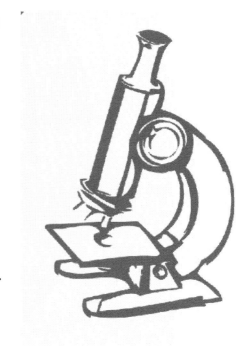

Which Will Freeze?

Pull out some salt, sugar, cornstarch, and flour. Compare the powders. Then, put 3 tablespoons of each one into four separate paper cups and label them. Add water and stir until the powders are dissolved.

Predict which {if any} of the water cups won't freeze because of the substances that have been added. Put the cups in the freezer.

Check on your cups in a few hours and see if your predictions were correct.

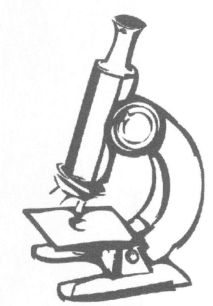

Chalking it Up

Fill a small bowl with vinegar and another with water. Compare the two liquids. What do they smell like? Look like? Taste like? How are they similar? How are they different?

Predict what will happen if you put a piece of chalk in each bowl. Write down your predictions. Then, place an identical piece of chalk in each bowl and record your observations. Now, predict what will happen if you leave each bowl alone for a week. Label the bowls and check back in a week.

How did your predictions compare with what actually happened?

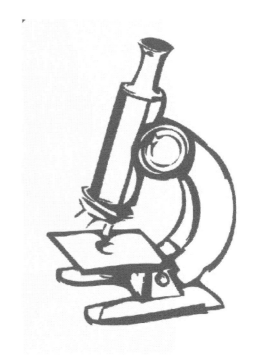

Water Drops

Compare wax paper, aluminum foil, plastic wrap, newspaper, and a paper towel. Which paper tears easiest? Which can stretch? Which is the loudest? Roughest? Smoothest?

Put a drop of water on each surface. Observe what happens on each. Draw or write your observations. Do you think different types of liquids would react differently than the water did? Try it again with different liquids and record your observations. Some ideas include — soapy water, cooking oil, apple juice, orange juice, paint, ink, etc.

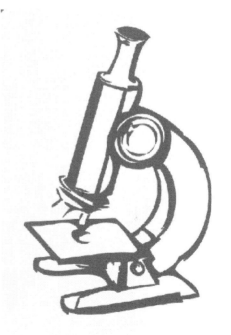

Whipped Cream Fun

You'll need a bowl of whipped cream, some raisins, pepper, and food coloring.

Scoop a bit of whipped cream into your hand. Observe its properties. How does it feel? What is it similar to? What does it taste like?

Observe the whipped cream and predict what will happen when you drop the raisins, pepper, and food coloring into the bowl. Do this, one item at a time, and observe the results.

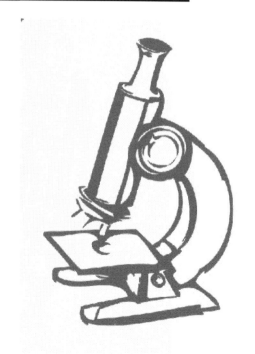

Now is the time to teach your children to wonder. Have them consider what would happen if the world were a little bit different. What if the sky were pink instead of blue? What if children made the rules and adults had to listen? Would things be better or worse? Why?

This kind of questioning and conversation may seem strange and pointless, but to a child it's fun. And, it serves a very important function. It teaches them to be flexible in their thinking and to look at things with fresh eyes.

One of my favorite books is <u>Frindle</u> by Andrew Clements. The main character discovers an interesting fact about the invention of new words and tries an experiment…a pen becomes a frindle. Something mundane… Something every day… Something normal… That something turns into an amazingly imaginative adventure. And shows kids that it's okay to think differently. In fact, different can be synonymous with extraordinary.

Let's encourage the extraordinary in your kids.

Colleen Kessler

Dressing Time

- How do you think shoes got their name?
- Why don't we say we "got pantsed" instead of "got dressed" when we're putting on pants and not dresses?
- How are a sweater and blanket alike? Different?
- What would cat socks look like?
- How is getting dressed like wrapping a gift? How is it different?
- Would it make sense for animals to wear shoes? Why? Why not?
- Which piece of clothing is the most important? Why?
- Pretend you own a strange bathing suit. What does it do that makes it strange?

Let's Eat

- What do kings prefer to eat for breakfast?
- What else is as cold as ice cream?
- What would be strange to put in your cereal?
- How are salt and sugar alike? How are they different?
- What is the best food to eat? The worst?
- Would you drink green milk? Why? Why not?
- Which food do you think is the most eaten food worldwide? Why?
- What do they serve at birthday parties on the planet Magilicutty?
- You are head chef at the most popular kid restaurant the world. What is your most popular meal?

What's Cooking

- What would Princess Aurora cook for Maleficent?
- How might a person get hurt while cooking?
- What do you think kitchens will look like a hundred years in the future?
- How are chopping vegetables and chopping wood alike? Different?
- What would you most like to learn to cook?
- Who should do the cooking in the house? Why?
- You have invented a new fast food. What is it?
- It was your turn to cook dinner, and things were going alright...at first. Then what happened?

Why do you think humans cook their food, but animals don't?

Play Time

- What famous person would you most like to be friends with? Why?
- What might a friend do that would hurt your feelings?
- Why do some people seem to have more friends than others?
- Why do friends sometimes fight with each other?
- How are a best friend and a teddy bear alike? Different?
- Do dogs make friends?
- What is the best thing a friend can do for another friend?
- You have been given the job of awarding the first-ever annual "Best Friend in the World" award. To whom will you give it? Why?

Cleaning Time

- Why do you think most people don't like to clean?
- Invent a game to make cleaning time fun.
- How could a messy house be unsafe?
- How are cleaning the house and cleaning yourself alike? Different?
- Should parents have to clean up messes made by their children? Why? Why not?
- What is the worst mess you have ever had to clean?
- You have just invented a toy-cleaner. What does it look like? What does it do?
- You just saw a TV commercial for a self-making bed. Convince your parents to buy it for you.

Bed Time

- Why do so many people read bedtime stories before bed?
- Where would be a strange place to sleep?
- Why do some people have trouble falling asleep?
- How are blankets and sheets alike? Different?
- Is it good to have a set bedtime? Why? Why not?
- Do you think dogs dream? What do they dream about?
- What was your best dream ever? Your worst nightmare ever?
- Do adult animals have bedtimes for their baby animals? How do they settle them?
- You have just invented a dream machine. Describe it.

Let's Go For a Ride

- What might be dangerous about a child yelling in a car?
- How would life be different if there were no cars?
- How are riding a bike and driving a car similar? Different?
- Do you like convertibles? Why? Why not?
- Should pets wear seat belts? Why? Why not?
- A new law has just passed allowing dogs to drive. What does a dog's car look like?
- Your car's horn doesn't honk. What sound do you imagine it makes instead?
- Will roads look the same in a hundred years? Why?

Grandparent's Day

- What do grandparents like best about being grandparents?
- What do you like best about your grandparents? Least?
- How are grandparents and parents similar? Different?
- How are your grandfather's clothes similar to your father's clothes? Different?
- Should grandparents live with their grandchildren? Why? Why not?
- What makes a good grandparent? Why?
- Pretend you are the grandparent and your grandchildren are coming for a visit. What will you do together?
- Your grandma just won the Boogie-Down-Grandma dance-off. What did it her routine look like?

At the Beach

- How do you think surfing was first invented?
- What might be very unusual to see at the beach?
- What could you do to make a sand castle extra special?
- How are waves and wind alike? Different?
- How are lifeguards and firefighters alike? Different?
- Do you enjoy the beach? Why? Why not?
- What might you pack for a beach picnic?
- Your mom just put a new sunblock on you. Something strange happened...what was it?
- A treasure chest washed up on the shore — what is in it?

At the Zoo

- Why do most kids enjoy going to the zoo?
- Why do giraffes have such long necks?
- Why are so many people afraid of snakes?
- How is an elephant's nose similar to a garden hose? Different?
- Could lions survive in the jungle after having lived in a zoo? Why? Why not?
- Would animals enjoy strolling through a human zoo?
- One of your favorite animals is having a conversation with you. Which animal is it? What are you talking about?
- The gorillas want something new to eat. What will you feed them?
- How did the ideas for zoos first come to be?

Celebrations are great ways to build family traditions and bring you closer together. Every day can be a celebration for a little one. Really. It doesn't have to be a holiday, but sometimes *pretending* that the holidays are here can be a great way to encourage imagination.

Making up your own holidays and events to celebrate can be fun, too. How about having a tea party to celebrate the first bud on a springtime tree? Or the first tadpole of the year? Or apple-picking season? Or national hot dog day? These traditions build strong family ties and foster the magic that IS childhood.

First Day of School

It's the first day of school — what will you do to celebrate?

• Bake a special cake?

• Wear a special outfit?

• Eat a cool lunch?

• Go out to dinner?

Imagine that you are a teacher and you walked into your classroom on the first day of school, but your students weren't children. What were they? How will you teach them? What subjects do they need to learn?

The First Day of Spring

It's the first day of spring — what will you do to celebrate?

- Plant some flowers?
- Take the day off?
- Plan a skit?
- Make a daisy crown?

Imagine that you are a spring fairy and are behind schedule in your seasonal preparations. What can you do to speed things up? What works? What goes wrong? Tell the story of your adventures.

Happy Birthday

It's your birthday — what will you do to celebrate?

• Open presents?

• Spend time with family or friends?

• Have a special meal?

• Go to a fun place?

Imagine that all your dreams come true. What is your perfect day? Describe it.

It's Halloween

It's Halloween — what will you do to celebrate?

• Wear a costume?

• Go out trick-or-treating?

• Stay at home and pass out candy?

• Go to a party?

Imagine that you get to throw the best Halloween party ever. Who will you invite? What snacks will you have? What will your theme be? What types of decorations will you have? What games will you play?

Thanksgiving Day

It's Thanksgiving — what will you do to celebrate?

• Help make a feast?

• Share what you are thankful for?

• Take a meal to someone who needs it?

• Go to a relative's home?

Imagine that you must cook Thanksgiving dinner all by yourself. How will you do it? What will you serve? Where will you get your food and how will you learn to prepare it? For how many people must you prepare?

Valentine's Day

It's Valentine's Day — what will you do to celebrate?

• Send a letter?

• Bake a treat for someone?

• Plan a special lunch?

• Spend time with a friend?

Imagine that you are planning a Valentine's Day dance for your friends. Where will you have it? How will you decorate? What type of music will you play? What food will you serve? What beverages? Will you play games? Will there be favors for dancers to take home?

Independence Day

It's Independence Day — what will you do to celebrate?

• Go to see fireworks?

• Watch a parade?

• Have a family picnic?

• Dress in red, white, and blue?

Imagine that you have a guest from out of the country staying with you. How will you explain Independence Day to him? What traditions does your town have to celebrate? Can you explain why they do that? What does your family do on this day? Why?

It's Summertime

It's the first day of summer — what will you do to celebrate?

- Run through a sprinkler?
- Make a "Bucket List?"
- Stay up all night?
- Camp in the backyard?

Imagine that you can do anything you want to do today. What would you do? What would you eat? What time would you get up? What time would you go to bed? With whom would you spend your day?

It's a Wedding

It's a wedding — what will you do to celebrate?

- Dress in fancy clothes?
- Drink sparkling cider from a champagne flute?
- Eat cake?
- Catch the bouquet?

Imagine that you are in a wedding. Who is getting married? What is your role? Are you happy to be in the wedding? Why? Why not? What are you wearing? What will you do all day? Will you dance? With whom?

Tea Party Time

It's a tea party — what will you do to celebrate?

• Dress up?

• Invite a friend?

• Bake a treat?

• Talk in a fancy voice?

Imagine that you are in a fancy hotel for high tea. You must be very polite. What are you wearing? Who are you with? What will you talk about? What are you being served? Describe your surroundings.

Colleen Kessler

In Conclusion

Remember, in the scheme of a lifetime, your kids are with you for such a short period of time. Make that time memorable for them – and for you. Live intentionally in every moment you can, even when you're having a bad day.

Being a parent is hard work, but raising those kids to be creative and critical thinkers doesn't have to be. In fact – it's child's play! If you're looking for more great ideas for encouraging your kids, head to www.RaisingLifelongLearners.com, where I share hands-on fun and learning ideas that are easy to replicate at home.

ABOUT THE AUTHOR

Colleen is a former teacher of gifted and talented children who prayed for nice, average kids, and never dreamed of leaving the classroom and thought homeschooling was weird. Since God has a sense of humor, she now finds herself homeschooling her four highly gifted and twice-exceptional children while working from home. She's published dozens of books for kids, parents, and teachers, and writes about homeschooling, parenting gifted kids, and hands-on learning and fun for all ages at

www.RaisingLifelongLearners.com

while trying desperately, and unsuccessfully, to stay one step ahead of her children {and their messes}. You can find her avoiding housework and the never-ending calls of "mo-om," by reading, writing, and sneaking chocolate from her hidden stash.

49529213R00043

Made in the USA
Columbia, SC
24 January 2019